EVOLUTION AND THE MODERN CHRISTIAN

EVOLUTION AND THE MODERN CHRISTIAN

by
Henry M. Morris

BAKER BOOK HOUSE
Grand Rapids, Michigan

ISBN: 0-8010-5881-3

First printing, August 1967
Second printing, September 1968
Third printing, December 1969
Fourth printing, September 1971
Fifth printing, March 1973

PHOTOLITHOPRINTED BY CUSHING - MALLOY, INC.
ANN ARBOR, MICHIGAN, UNITED STATES OF AMERICA
1 9 7 3

PREFACE

Young people in practically all public schools today and many of those in private schools are continuously and increasingly being indoctrinated with the evolutionary philosophy. Whether this indoctrination is overt and insistent, as in most high school biology texts and courses, or subtle and sublimated, as in the very methodology of modern educationism, it is surely very real and effective. It begins in the lowest grades, where children are taught about the great dinosaurs who roamed the earth a hundred million years ago and about the primitive, ape-like cave men who accidentally discovered fire and other rudiments of civilization long before the dawn of history. Social, and cultural evolution is stressed in the various courses in history and social studies throughout junior high and senior high. General science and physics courses commonly include the latest speculations on the supposed evolution of the universe and of matter. Literature selections in the English courses often seem calculated to promote the mis-named "new morality" which is the logical product of an intellectual commitment to the idea of evolution.

The truths of Christian theism and Biblical Christianity, on the other hand, are increasingly being denied, even ridiculed, or (which is worst of all) ignored as irrelevant, in our entire educational system. The much-discussed U. S. Supreme Court decisions relating to the religion-in-public-schools issue are not the cause, but rather one effect, of this situation. The evolutionary philosophy stemming from Darwinism and its predecessors in the nineteenth century, implemented by the evolutionistic and socialistic minded architects of modern education (such as John Dewey and his colleagues, and even Horace Mann before them), has culminated in a vast educational complex of diverse pedagogical methods and "learning experiences," multitudinous "life-oriented" specialized courses and extra-curricular activities, along with much admittedly solid and valuable curricular content in the basic intellectual disciplines — but all woven together in a naturalistic and evolutionary framework of tremendous influence and power.

It is therefore of little wonder that most high school students nowadays are thoroughly committed to an evolutionary faith when they graduate. The writer had the saddening experience of speaking very recently to a young people's group in a large, old-line Protestant church in a traditionally conservative community, on the general subject of the scientific validity of the Bible. The question-and-answer period following the talk quickly revealed not only that most of these high-schoolers were believers in total evolution but that many also rejected the inspiration of the Bible and deity of Christ, and some even the idea of a future life and a personal God.

Now the most amazing thing about this whole state of affairs is the absurdity and impossibility of the very concept of evolution! That a theory which is so utterly devoid of any legitimate scientific proof could have attained such a position of universal power and prestige in the name of science is surely a remarkable commentary on human nature. Whether the explanation lies in some monumental web of intellectual conspiracy or merely in man's enormous capacity for egocentric self-deception, the simple fact is that the evolutionary philosophy is both totally false and almost totally successful.

The Christian school movement is a partial answer to this situation and should be supported by Christian people to the greatest extent possible. Young people can and should be taught all their school subjects in the true framework of Biblical creationism, and many Christian schools have had notable success in this direction.

However, it is a painfully realistic fact that not more than a minute fraction of the world's youth, even of those from truly Christian homes and churches, can ever be taught in a genuinely Christian and creationistic school system. We need urgently to reach the host of others with literature which will in some way open their minds and hearts to the true Biblical cosmology.

This small book has been prepared with this one need primarily in mind. It is intentionally brief, in order to minimize both the cost and the time required for reading it. It is sufficiently non-technical so that no intelligent high school or college student should have difficulty in understanding it, but, at the same time, there has been no attempt to "popularize" its style or vocabulary. The writer respects the intellectual capacity and integrity of young people too much for this kind of device.

The book hopefully may serve as a suitable text for Sunday School classes, study courses, summer camp workshops and similar organized young people's groups. In addition, it can easily be read straight through by any interested young person, and it is hoped that means can be found for wide distribution of the book on an individual basis to high school and college students.

The writer has a real interest in young people, and knows something of the tremendous pressures to which they are subjected in these critical days. He is especially thankful for his own three fine sons (Henry, John, Andrew) and three lovely daughters (Kathleen, Mary Ruth, Rebecca), all of whom are either in or have recently completed the difficult teen-age years, and all of whom are Bible-believing Christians. It is to them and their friends this little book is dedicated.

Thanks are also expressed to the following: Mr. Norman Jerome, of the American Sunday School Union, whose suggestion stimulated the writer to begin the book; Dr. John C. Whitcomb, Jr., of Grace Seminary in Winona Lake, Indiana, who reviewed the manuscript; the writer's mother, Mrs. I. H. Morris, who typed the manuscript; and the publisher, Mr. Charles H. Craig, whose advice and cooperation on the project have been most helpful.

Henry M. Morris
Blacksburg, Virginia
June 1967

CONTENTS

Chapter One

THE MEANING OF EVOLUTION

"Why should Christians be concerned with evolution? Assuming that God is really the one who began it all, what difference does it make whether He created the world instantaneously or allowed everything to develop gradually over long ages? Isn't it more important for the Christian to be involved in present-day issues and to concentrate on living a fruitful Christian life than it is to worry and argue about the distant past?"

These objections and others like them are frequently heard in modern Christian circles, especially among high school and college young people. On the surface they seem to make good sense. Surely one's present activity and future destiny are much more important than his primeval origin. Or so it would seem.

But when one begins to study the question, not just *on* the surface but *beneath* the surface as well, he soon realizes that this problem of origins is not a secondary issue at all but rather one of profound importance. One's beliefs concerning origins will inevitably condition his beliefs concerning intrinsic meanings and ultimate destinies. The modern intellectual and social climate has been in large measure the product of a century or more of evolutionary philosophy. The various modern issues confronting young people — problems of war and peace, racial conflicts, the so-called "new" morality, nationalism versus world federalism, communism, and others — are all closely related to the old conflict between creationism and evolutionism.

Importance of Evolution

A recent manifesto,* circulated by world-renowned geneticist, H. J. Muller, and signed by 177 American biologists, asserts unequivocally that the organic evolution of all living things, man included, from primitive life forms and even ultimately from non-living materials, is a fact of science as well established as the fact that the earth is round! The widely-accepted Biological Sciences Curriculum Study high school biology textbooks, financed by the National Science Foundation, have organized their entire treatment of biological science around the assumed evolutionary framework of life history. In fact, almost all the books and articles on biology published by secular publishers for at least the past two generations have been written from evolutionary presuppositions.

The obvious fact that most biologists are committed to the evolutionary philosophy is, of course, a major factor in the reluctance of young Christians and of educated people generally to take a stand in favor of Biblical creationism. In this modern scientific age, one just does not oppose science!

Furthermore, this commitment to evolution is not confined to biologists. Most astronomers, for example, assume that the universe is continually evolving, and much of their work is directed to an understanding of "stellar

---

*H. J. Muller: "Is Biological Evolution a Principle of Nature that Has Been Well Established by Science?" (Privately duplicated and distributed by author), May 2, 1966.

evolution." The geologist utilizes evolution as the main tool in his interpretation of the earth's physical history. Even physicists and chemists often think in terms of a primeval evolution of the chemical elements and molecules from basic particles.

But if the concept of evolution is widespread in the physical and biological sciences, it is even more influential in the social sciences and the humanities, and it is these fields of study that most directly impinge on man's daily thoughts and activities. Sociology, psychology, economics, literature, the fine arts — these and others of the "liberal arts" have direct bearing on our everyday concerns and decisions, our morals and recreations.

It is thus highly significant that these "social sciences," as well as the "humanities," are now nearly always taught in an evolutionary framework. It is generally assumed nowadays that the Biblical record of origins is "pre-scientific," at best only allegorical and certainly not literal and historical. The Biblical teachings of man's responsibility to his Creator, the fact of sin and the fall of man, and the necessity of redemption and regeneration, have all been set aside in favor of the concepts of evolutionary progress, of universal struggle and natural selection, of man's genetic kinship with the animals, of a "this-life-only" approach to social problems, and of humanistic, rather than theistic, criteria for decision-making in every area of life.

Nor is this evolutionary emphasis confined to the secular realm. The theology of most religious denominations has long since been adapted to the perspective of evolution, especially among religious "liberals." The concept of theistic evolution (or, what amounts to almost the same thing, "progressive creation") is widely accepted, according to which evolution is God's "method of creation." The Genesis record is not considered to be actual history, but rather a "cosmogonic myth," or perhaps an "allegory" or "poem." In fact, the entire Bible is taken simply as one religious book among others, the record of the religious and cultural evolution of the Hebrews and early Christians. It is said to contain much of lasting moral and religious value but also much which is unacceptable in the enlightened world of the twentieth century. The "liberal" Christian, therefore, is concerned much more with the continuing evolution of the social order (e.g., the labor movement, civil rights, welfare legislation, etc.) than he is with the defense and propagation of the gospel.

The evolution virus has infected even the sphere of evangelical Christianity. Especially is this true among the "new evangelicals," who have been diligently laboring for the past quarter of a century to render Biblical Christianity more palatable to modern tastes. Many once strongly fundamental schools, seminaries, publications, and even mission boards have in the past decade or so accepted evolution in greater or lesser degree and have sought to accommodate the Biblical record to this assumption.

But of special significance is the fact that the various movements and philosophies of the present day which have been in formal opposition to Biblical Christianity have all based their claims for validity on the supposed historical fact of evolutionary struggle and progress. This is especially true for the systems of Communism and Nazism, for the amoral psychologies of behaviorism and Freudianism, and for the religious philosophies of existentialism and the "death of God."

For these, among many other, reasons, it ought to be obvious that no serious Christian can properly ignore the evolution question. It is not some sort of peripheral issue of little relevance to the demands of the Christian life, but rather it has profound effect, whether he realizes it or not, in every area of his life. It is not too much to say that the evolutionary philosophy, consistently accepted and applied, squarely contradicts Biblical Christianity in every essential feature. It is therefore extremely important that Christians, especially young people, be well informed on the evidences for and against evolution, as well as its significance in light of the Biblical revelation.

The Evidential Basis

One would suppose that a theory of such universal acceptance and influence must be supported by innumerable and incontrovertible evidences. This, indeed, is what its proponents claim.

However, when we seek to examine these evidences in detail, we begin to encounter problems. Professor Muller in the manifesto mentioned previously says concerning these evidences for evolution:

> It would be impossible in a few hours to make clear the significance and the weight of this great mass of extraordinary and intricate findings, to persons not already possessed of a considerable biological background. In fact, even they could hardly grasp them in full without long and deep study, preferably extending over years.

If this judgment is true, then, of course, ordinary laymen, without the advantages of years of graduate work and deep study in the biological sciences, could not hope to evaluate the significance of the proffered evidences for evolution. Consequently we are supposed to leave decisions of this sort up to the experts. If Dr. Muller and his colleagues say evolution is true, then it must be true. They say so; it is presumptuous of us to raise questions! If this means that the Bible is false, that the God-idea is dead, that Communism is the next stage of evolutionary history, and that men are merely animals who have learned to understand and control their own future evolution, then so be it. The authorities have decreed what we are to believe and that is that!

Fortunately, however, biological textbooks commonly do at least enumerate and briefly discuss the various lines of evidence that supposedly prove evolution to be a fact. Thus, even though we have been forewarned that we are not qualified to weigh the merits of these evidences, we can at least ascertain what they are. The listings vary somewhat from one book to another but the following constitute at least the main lines of evidence.

(1) *Evidence from Classification.* The fact that it is possible to arrange the various kinds of plants and animals into categories of species, genera, families, orders, etc., is supposed to suggest that there are genetic relationships between them.

(2) *Evidence from Comparative Anatomy.* Similarities in skeletal structure, such as between apes and men or horses and elephants, are assumed to imply evolutionary kinship.

(3) *Evidence from Embryology.* Similarities in embryos of different kinds of animals and the supposed "evolutionary" growth of the embryo into the adult animal are taken as evidence that the animals are related and that they have passed through an analogous evolutionary development into their present forms during the geologic past.

(4) *Evidence from Biochemistry.* The fact that all living organisms are composed of certain basic chemical substances (amino acids, proteins, deoxyribose nucleic acid, etc.) is supposed to prove that all living organisms have a common ancestry.

(5) *Evidence from Physiology.* Certain similarities in physiological factors, especially blood precipitates, and of behavior characteristics are offered as further evidences of genetic kinships.

(6) *Evidence from Geographical Distribution.* The tendency of certain kinds of plants and animals to vary in character with geographic location, and especially to assume distinct characteristics when isolated from similar populations in other regions, is presumed to suggest evolution.

(7) *Evidence from Vestigal Organs.* Certain supposedly useless structures and organs (e.g., the appendix in man) are believed to represent "vestiges" of characters which were once useful and functional in a previous evolutionary stage.

(8) *Evidence from Breeding Experiments.* The many new varieties of plants and animals that have been developed by hybridization and other breeding techniques are taken as indicative of the evolutionary potential implicit in living organisms, which presumably has been realized over the geologic ages through the mechanism of "natural selection," just as "artificial selection" has been used by man to develop new varieties.

(9) *Evidence from Mutations.* The observed fact that entirely new varieties or species suddenly

appear in a particular organism (or "popula-tion" of organisms) is offered as the best present-day visual proof of evolution; these new characteristics are called "mutations" and it is said that, if these turn out to be favorable, they will be preserved by natural selection and thus contribute to the long-term evolutionary process.

(10) *Evidence from Paleontology.* The fossil record of former living things, as preserved in the sedi-mentary rocks of the earth's crust, is offered as an actual documented history of organic evolution, with the degree of complexity of the fossils supposedly increasing with the passage of geologic time, thus marking the gradual de-velopment of the present organic world from primitive and simple beginnings about a billion years ago.

With these ten major lines of evidence, taken from ten important fields of science, it does seem at first that the evidence for evolution is indeed very strong.

However, upon closer examination, it is evident that these are all circumstantial, rather than demonstrative, evidences. It is therefore possible that some other ex-planation can account for them as well as, or better than, the theory of evolution.

Thus the first five evidences listed above are merely evidences of similarities of one kind or another. Such similarities can surely be understood in terms of creation by a common Creator, even better than in terms of evolutionary kinships.

The next four evidences call attention to the fact that certain biological changes can and do take place. But again, this obvious fact can be explained equally well in terms of the special creation of all the basic "kinds" of organisms, with provision in their respective genetic structures for such variations as might be required in the future for adaptation to different environments.

It is only the last of the evidences, that from paleontology, that purports to present actual historical proof of evolution on a large scale. But even this evidence, which is by far the most important of all the supposed evidences for evolution, is also really only circumstantial in nature. The fact that two different assemblages of organisms may have lived during two different epochs of geologic history does not by any means *prove* that one group evolved into the other group.

Thus none of the ten evidences necessarily prove evolution. And when we examine the respective evidences still more closely, as we shall do in later chapters, we shall find that there are almost insuperable difficulties with the evolutionary explanation of *each* of the different evidences. They can all be understood much better in terms of special creation than in terms of evolution.

The belligerent commitment to the evolutionary philosophy on the part of so many intellectuals today is, therefore, not due to the idea that there is no other satisfying explanation of the biological world but rather due to the fact that they *prefer* to believe in evolution! The only alternative to an evolutionary origin for the universe and its life is that of creation. And since creation is assumed to be outside the sphere of scientific study, evolution is chosen as the only alternative.

As a matter of fact, the entire question of origins (whether by creation or evolution) is really outside the domain of science, not being susceptible to scientific experimentation and analysis. Knowledge of origins must come from outside of science — it is, therefore, not really a scientific question at all. This will be discussed more fully later. Suffice it to say for the present that only the Creator — God Himself — can tell us what is the truth about the origin of all things. And this He has done, in the Bible, if we are willing simply to believe what He has told us.

Chapter Two

SCIENTIFIC WEAKNESSES OF EVOLUTION

As noted in the first chapter, the study of origins does not really fall within the domain of science at all. Science, in the strict sense, means "knowledge," and therefore must necessarily be based on actual experimental measurements and analyses. Since it is completely impossible to make any actual measurements or experiments on the origins of the universe or life or the various kinds of life, it is therefore also impossible for *science*, as such, to tell us about these things.

However, it is possible for us to make observations concerning things as they *now* exist and to make experiments which will enable us to understand *present* natural processes; these are the proper spheres of descriptive science and empirical science, respectively. On the basis of such observations and experiments we may then develop hypotheses to explain how things got that way. With respect to ultimate origins, it would never be possible to *prove*, scientifically, which hypothesis (i.e., evolution or special creation) is right.

The most that could ever be done is to make as thorough an examination of the evidence as possible and then to make a judgment as to which hypothesis yields the most probable explanation of the data. This judgment is bound to be subjective to some extent and, as a matter of fact, even in part based on spiritual considerations and preferences. Our purpose in this chapter will be to show that the so-called evidences for evolution can also be explained, at least equally well, in terms of special creation. The decision between the two hypotheses, then, becomes mainly a moral and spiritual decision instead of a scientific decision.

The Significance of Similarities

The first five of the evidences for evolution, as enumerated in the first chapter, were based on resemblances between different kinds of plants and animals. These similarities were taken as proof of evolutionary kinship. On the other hand, the creationist says that they speak rather of a common Designer and thus tend to indicate creation instead of evolution.

In fact, upon examining the evidences in some detail, it becomes evident that the evolutionary explanation involves many contradictions, hypotheses within hypotheses, and innumerable "leaps of faith" to account for the data. The concept of creation, on the other hand, is very simple and straightforward, requiring only faith in an omnipotent God and His divine revelation to account quite easily for all the data.

For example, consider the evidence from classification, the arrangement of living forms into kingdoms, phyla, classes, orders, families, genera, species and races, in order of increasing specialization. This arrangement is considered by the evolutionist to indicate also an increasing closeness in evolutionary relationship.

On the other hand, if all organisms are truly related by evolutionary descent from a common ancestor, it is strange that any kind of classification system would be possible at all! There should rather be a universal and gradual inter-grading of all kinds of creatures into each other. Why, for example, can all animals be divided into the Protozoa (one-celled animals) and Metazoa (many-celled animals)? Why are there no two-celled and three-celled animals? Why are there many varieties of dogs and many varieties of cats, but no animals intermediate between cats and dogs? Or between apes and men? The fact that there are such clear-cut gaps between the various families, and even to considerable extent between genera and species (and that these same gaps exist in the fossil record) is strong evidence against the evolutionist explanation.

What about the evidences from comparative anatomy and physiology? On the assumption of creation, it is reasonable that there would be resemblances between creatures and that these resemblances would be stronger between those creatures living in similar environments and with similar physiologic functions to fulfill. One could hardly imagine any more probable an arrangement than now prevails, if the origin of all things actually were special creation.

The really remarkable thing, if evolution is true, is that there are so many *differences* among creatures. If all organisms originated from a common ancestor, and if all subsequent forms have inhabited the same world under fairly restricted environmental conditions, how is it possible to explain the almost infinite variety of plants and animals in the present world? Far more probable, under the hypothesis of evolutionary development, would it be for all modern creatures to have essentially the *same* anatomy and physiology!

The same argument applies to similarities in embryological development. Since most animal embryos develop under somewhat similar environmental conditions until birth from an initial union of two microscopic germ cells, it is reasonable that they would have a somewhat standardized appearance for a time until reaching a stage of size and growth at which the appropriate specialized features of the particular animal could begin to develop. These similarities are somewhat superficial at best, since at no time after conception is there any uncertainty as to what type of creature will eventually develop from the embryo.

We need not even discuss the old idea that "ontogeny recapitulates phylogeny" (that is, that the various stages in embryonic growth recap in miniature and abbreviated form the evolutionary development of the particular species). No competent embryologist believes this somewhat bizarre notion any more. There are innumerable exceptions to this so-called "rule." As a matter of fact, every stage in the development of every embryo is quite essential to its own development, and thus in no way is it merely a pointless repetition of some hypothetical evolutionary history.

There is currently much emphasis being placed on molecular biology, because of its insights into the biochemical nature of the genetic structure of the germ cell, and the mechanisms employed in reproduction and the transmission of heredity. The fact that all living things contain complex molecules of D.N.A. (deoxyribosenucleic acid) in their germ cells and that this substance seems to control the determination of heredity is taken as proof of a common evolutionary origin of all things, presumably beginning with D.N.A. by itself in some primeval ocean. Various amino acids, enzymes and other proteins are also present in all living organisms.

This, of course, is essentially the same argument as the argument from other forms of similarity and, like them, can obviously also be understood in terms of a common Designer.

Again the differences are really of far greater significance than the similarities. In spite of the common possession of D.N.A. by all organisms, the hereditary "information" for each is uniquely "coded" in the structure of the particular D.N.A. molecules so that only that structure which is already present in the parent organism can be transmitted to its progeny. Or, putting it in another way, the genetic structure of the germ cell of each creature is unique to that creature, and nothing can be transmitted to the descendant which is not at least implicitly present in the ancestor. There are great numbers of "genes" (or D.N.A. molecules) in each germ cell, and these can be arranged in various ways to permit a wide range of variation in the individual members of a basic "kind" of plant or animal, but the possible range of variation is nevertheless limited to the basic genetic framework of that particular "kind." Thus nothing really *new* can be added in the process of reproduction. All the "information" for the development of each particular organism was already "encoded" in the D.N.A. of its parent. They *must* reproduce "after their kinds."

The Nature of Biologic Change

The four evolutionary evidences of geographical distribution, vestigial organs, breeding experiments, and mutations all point to certain actual changes in particular species. These changes are related respectively to geographical isolation, to disuse, to artificial breeding techniques, and to natural modifications in genetic structure.

There is no question that such changes actually do occur in the biological world. No intelligent creationist seeks to argue for the fixity of *species* or of any other arbitrary unit of classification. He does maintain, however, that there is no evidence of change beyond certain limits and that these limits, whatever they may eventually turn out to be genetically, will be basically the same as the concept of the created "kinds" of the first chapter of Genesis.

Closer inspection of such changes in biological organisms will reveal that they are of two basic types. For purposes of discussion, we shall call these variations and mutations. Variations are the normal changes that occur within the framework of the basic kinds. No two individuals are exactly alike, even when born of the same parents. The genetic system permits a wide variety of specific features (eye color, height, shape of skull, etc.) within the limits of the particular kind. These characteristics vary in accordance with the Mendelian laws of heredity. Depending on factors such as possible isolation and inbreeding, some of these characteristics may become more or less fixed and a definite "race" established.

Although the number of varieties or races that may be established from an original kind is undoubtedly quite large, it is clear that there are definite limits to this process and thus that ordinary variation, or even speciation, has no true evolutionary significance. New varieties can be established, but not new kinds.

It is sometimes possible for a completely new characteristic to appear in a particular kind of organism, outside the scope of that organism's usual range of variation. This phenomenon is known as a *mutation*. These are considered to be very important biological events. In fact, it is now almost universally believed by evolutionists that mutations, preserved by natural selection if they are beneficial in the struggle for existence, provide the basic mechanism of organic evolution. This is the essence of "neo-Darwinism" or the so-called "modern evolutionary synthesis," especially when emphasis is placed on "populations" of organisms, rather than individuals.

Mutations definitely do occur, and they are definitely hereditable, entering into the genetic pool with other Mendelian characteristics. And it does seem reasonable that, if a particular mutant character turns out to be favorable and to make its possessor better qualified to compete in the surrounding environment in the struggle for existence, it would have a real "survival value." Perhaps, then, over the ages an accumulation of such favorable mutations preserved by natural selection might result in a new, better-equipped "kind" of organism.

But there are at least two insuperable difficulties associated with the mutation theory, and these are such as to leave the entire concept in the domain of wishful evolutionary thinking rather than in that of experimental science.

One difficulty is that all actually observed mutations are relatively small and insignificant; that is, they are *micro*-mutations. An accumulation of literally millions of such micro-mutations would be necessary to change one basic "kind" of plant or animal into another. And the insoluble problem which this idea entails, even if unlimited time were available for the process, is that every organism is a functioning whole as it stands, with innumerable essential inter-relationships among its various organs and structures. It is impossible to imagine, much less observe, how such complex systems as these could have been developed by infinitesimally slow processes of minute mutations. What survival value would an incipient eye, or heart, or liver, for example, have in the functioning of some primitive organism? Such organs would be useless, and even harmful, if not fully developed and functioning from the beginning.

An even more serious difficulty is the fact that practically all *observed* mutations are harmful, and usually even fatal, to the creature experiencing them. Truly beneficial mutations are so rarely observed, and even these are so questionable, as to leave their very existence still in doubt. Even evolutionary geneticists readily acknowledge that at least 99.9 per cent of all observed mutations are harmful.

The reason that this is so is quite obvious. The genetic system of any organism is a highly complex, delicately functioning, intricately adapted system for transmitting the hereditary nature and characteristics of the species and the particular parents. A mutation represents a *random change* in this highly organized system, brought about by penetration of the system by some intruding agent, such as radiation, powerful chemicals, or physical disturbances of some kind or another. When the genetic system is thus disturbed and changed, it naturally produces some effect on the creature resulting from it, and this effect would almost certainly be harmful. Any *random* change in a highly organized system has only an infinitesimal chance of improving the functioning of the system.

But even if this infinitesimal chance actually were successful and the mutant organism did turn out to be better adapted in its environment than its parents, this still would be only one out of the millions of such mutations needed to develop a really new "kind." The chance for still another favorable mutation occurring in the same species is yet smaller. That is, the chance of a successful random change occurring in a system decreases as the complexity of the system increases. The number of uncounted billions upon billions of favorable mutations required to develop the amazing variety and intricate complexity of the present organic world out of some hypothetical primitive common ancestor is beyond our powers to calculate or even to imagine.

Some evolutionists have postulated "*macro*-mutations" as a possible way out of this blind alley. This would be something like an eye suddenly developing in fully functioning form in one single mutation! The problem with this suggestion, of course, is that such macro-mutations have never been observed experimentally, nor is there any known biological mechanism which would permit them.

Some evolutionists point to the change in colors of moth species from light to dark with the coming of the industrial revolution in England, or to the development of penicillin-resistant bacteria and pesticide-resistant insects as examples of effective micro-mutations, which illustrate the basic mechanism of evolution. Such examples are, of course, not to the point. At best they are only micro-mutations and produce what amounts to new varieties (or species) within the same kind. Furthermore, it is uncertain whether they represent true mutations at all. It is equally likely that they represent possible genetic varieties which were implicitly present all the time in the gene pool, requiring only a brief exposure of the population to natural selection in the changed environment to make them predominant. Development of adaptive varieties of this type does not require long ages but is accomplished quite rapidly and seems most reasonably to be a divine provision within the complex genetic structures of the original "kinds."

Thus neither normal variation, which operates about a fixed center, nor true mutation, which operates in the direction of deterioration of the stock, represents legitimate evidences of real evolution.

Chapter Three

THE FOSSIL RECORD

Of the ten evolutionary evidences cited earlier, the first nine were seen to be strictly circumstantial in nature. Five of them merely involved anatomical and physiological resemblances which can be explained much more reasonably in terms of creation by a common Designer. Four involved evidences of actual biological changes, but these were seen to be either adaptive variations around the fixed center of each basic "kind" or deteriorative changes.

The tenth and last evidence for evolution is that derived from paleontology, which is the study of fossilized remains of organisms which have been buried and preserved in the sedimentary rocks of the earth's crust. This evidence is different from the others in that it purports to show the actual history of evolution rather than its present results and mechanisms. In fact, evolutionists frequently state that even though we may not understand yet just *how* evolution functions, the historical *fact* of evolution is proved by the fossil record.

The Geological Ages

The framework of interpretation for the fossil record consists of the so-called "geologic ages." The science of geology (meaning "study of the earth") deals with the physical and chemical structure of the crust of the earth, the forces and processes which are acting upon that crust, and the history of the earth's development into its present form. Most geologists (though not all) have decided that the earth is very old, perhaps about five billion years. The first 80 per cent of this vast period of time is supposed to have had no organic life at all, and this period is now evidenced mostly by the crystalline rocks of what is known as the "basement complex."

Primitive living material is assumed to have evolved from complex chemicals in the primitive ocean about a billion or more years ago. The sedimentary rocks deposited on top of the basement rocks contain fossil remains of animals and plants which have supposedly gradually evolved from those first organisms. The "geologic column" is the accumulation of sedimentary rocks (with occasional igneous rock "intrusions"), with their contained fossils, which have been piled up since that time.

This geologic column has been subdivided into various segments marking off the different geologic ages. The main divisions are the Paleozoic ("ancient life"), the Mesozoic ("intermediate life") and the Cenozoic ("recent life"). Each of these is extensively further subdivided but we could say, very approximately, that the Paleozoic was characterized especially by marine life and amphibians, the Mesozoic by reptiles, and the Cenozoic by birds and mammals.

The supposedly very ancient Paleozoic rocks thus contain relatively simple organisms, the more recent Mesozoic rocks contain more advanced types and the young Cenozoic rocks contain the most highly developed and specialized forms. This progression is thus offered as actual documentary evidence that evolution *has* occurred over the geologic ages, whether or not we understand *how* it occurred. This is certainly the most impressive and significant of all the proffered evidences for evolution and requires the most thorough evaluation.

Gaps in the Record

There are at least two major objections to this line of proof. In the first place, even assuming that the geological ages are actually correct as presented, the same basic gaps between different kinds of creatures that we have seen to exist in the present biological world persist in the fossil record. There are *still* no organisms intermediate between the protozoa and metazoa, between the dog and the cat, between the horse and elephant. There have been many extinct species found, of course, but these all represent basically either additional varieties of present kinds of creatures or else examples of basic kinds which have themselves become extinct (such as the various kinds of dinosaurs).

All of the present orders, classes and phyla appear quite suddenly in the fossil record, without indications of the evolving lines from which they presumably developed. The same is largely true even for most families and genera. There are literally an innumerable host of "missing links" in the record.

This phenomenon cannot possibly be due to the "incompleteness of the fossil record," as Darwin and others have claimed in the past. The paleontological record is instead quite ample to represent the true state of the ancient world. Most individual species of fossil plants and animals have been collected in considerable numbers, but the hypothetical intermediate species have never been represented in the collections at all! The occasional suggested examples of missing links (such as the famous

archaeopteryx — supposedly linking the birds and reptiles) can usually be recognized on closer study to represent merely another type of one of the basic kinds it
supposedly links (the archaeopteryx was a true bird, by
any reasonable definition, with feathers and warm blood).

At best, therefore, the fossil record can suggest only
that different kinds of organisms originated at different
times in earth history but not that they evolved out of
each other! If continuous evolution is a universal law of
nature, as the evolutionist claims, then there should be an
abundance of evidences of continuity and transition between all the kinds of organisms involved in the process,
both in the present world and in the fossil record. Instead
we find great gaps between all the basic kinds, and essentially the same gaps in the fossil record that exist in
the modern world.

Reasoning in a Circle

The second major objection to the proof of evolution
from paleontology is that the very structure of the geologic ages is itself based on the assumption of evolution.
Thus, the main *proof* of evolution is based on the *assumption* of evolution!

The rock formations of the earth do not come equipped
with corner stones certifying their assumed dates of formation. How, then, do geologists determine the age of
a particular rock and whether one rock is older than
another?

The answer, somewhat oversimplified but nevertheless
fundamentally correct, is that the date is determined by
the fossils it contains. If the fossils are only simple marine
organisms, then it must be dated in one of the Paleozoic
systems; if it contains fossil mammals, then it must be

Cenozoic. In other words, the assumption of an ages-long evolutionary development of the organic world is the basic key for identifying and dating the various components of the geologic column.

It is true, of course, that other factors (e.g., the physical characteristics of the rocks, the superposition of one layer over another, etc.) are also used for correlating and distinguishing different formations in any given locality. But whenever there is any conflict between the physical and paleontological evidence, the paleontological evidence always governs. And when it comes to correlating rocks in one region with those in some distant region, the evolutionary succession of fossils is always the main criterion.

This is obviously a flagrant case of circular reasoning and thus is not a legitimate proof. Evolution is assumed in building up the geological column, superimposing rock systems from different regions all over the world on top of each other. Then the column thus constructed, with its arbitrary geologic ages, is formally offered as the one best documentary proof of the *historic fact* of evolution!

This would not be so bad if it were fully self-consistent, that is, if the small portion of the geologic column found in each locality were always in agreement with the column as a whole (the entire geologic column is well over a hundred miles thick, whereas the sedimentary crust at any one locality is never more than a very small fraction of this). However, there are great numbers of contradictions and inconsistencies found everywhere! Hundreds of sites are known, for example, where formations which are "old" (that is, which contain primitive fossils) directly overlie formations which are "young" (containing more "recent" types of organisms). Often the contact line between such anomalous formations is essentially horizontal and undisturbed, looking for all the world like they had been deposited normally in just the order in which they are found. Yet the evolutionary succession requires that they be explained away somehow in terms of great earth upheavals which "overturn" or "overthrust" the original deposits into their present anomalous order!

Thus we are well justified in lodging a double indictment against the paleontological evidence for evolution. Not only do the fossil assemblages as presented via the standard geologic ages fail to prove evolution because of the innumerable "gaps" which still remain in them, but also the very existence of the geologic ages themselves is brought into serious question by the fact that the assumption of evolution is absolutely necessary to establish them!

Geologic Catastrophism

The question may now be asked: if the fossil record does not tell the history of evolution on the earth, just what does it tell? If the earth is really five billion years old and the fossil-bearing rocks perhaps one billion years old, there at least seems to have been *time* for evolution. But if all things were specially created, why would God have stretched the process out over such a long period, when man himself would be only a relatively late addition to the cosmos?

We have seen that the *relative* ages of the different rocks, as determined by the fossils, are not really valid. It may well be also that the *absolute* age of the earth has been grossly over-estimated.

Actually, the earth only appears to be very old if we make the assumption of *uniformity*, that is, if we assume that the great thicknesses of sedimentary rocks on the earth's crust have been formed by the same geologic processes (weathering, erosion, streamflow, silting, etc.) that now operate, and at essentially the same rates. It obviously would take many millions of years for a river to deposit sediments in its delta which, when combined with the processes of earth subsidence, compaction and lithification, would eventually result in a column of sedimentary rocks several miles thick.

But this philosophy, known as *uniformitarianism*, cannot be proved to be true. There is no way of knowing that these rates, or even the processes themselves, have always been the same as now. This is strictly and entirely an assumption.

The same rocks can also be explained, and even more easily so, on the basis of *catastrophism*. Thus, great floods, volcanic eruptions, landslides, earthquakes, and the like, can and do accomplish vast amounts of geologic "work" quickly and catastrophically. Long ages are not necessary. Furthermore, it is quite possible that such geologic catastrophes occurred more frequently and on a larger scale in the past, when the earth was younger, than they do at present. It is obvious that reliable calculations of geologic age can only be made if the uniformity assumption is valid, and such an assumption can *never* be *proved* valid!

As a matter of fact, the rocks themselves give abundant proof that uniformitarianism is not true. There are vast regions of volcanic rocks, for example, that cannot possibly be accounted for on the basis of present types of volcanic activity. There are great thicknesses of alluvial deposits of far greater size than modern streams could ever accumulate. Continent-size glaciers are necessary to account for the glacial deposits of the northern hemisphere, and these are certainly incommensurate with any type of modern glacier. Great folds and thrusts and faults, found all over the world, testify of ancient earth

˙ movements of size and power far eclipsing anything ever experienced in the modern world.

Even the fossil deposits which form the very basis for geologic dating must have been deposited catastrophically, or else the fossils would never have been preserved at all. Rapid burial is necessary if a fossil is to be formed; otherwise the organism would quickly disappear because of scavengers or decay. The uncounted millions upon millions of fossil organisms buried in the rocks of the earth's crust therefore testify unequivocally to the fact of catastrophism, rather than uniformitarianism, as the proper key to a real understanding of geologic history.

Biblical Catastrophism

The next question to be considered has to do, therefore, with the nature and number of such catastrophes. Once the principle of catastrophism is admitted, the door is admittedly opened to all sorts of speculative theories. Were there many catastrophes at different times in geologic history or only one? Is catastrophism to be postulated in terms of colliding planets, meteoritic impacts, cometary phenomena, slipping crusts, shifting poles, nuclear explosions, sinking continents, or what? Obviously, the field is wide open, and many geologic phenomena can apparently be explained in terms of each of the various theories of catastrophism.

But there is no need to speculate. Nearly all ancient nations and tribes have traditions of a tremendous upheaval at the dawn of human history which destroyed the ancient world and through which only a small remnant of men and animals survived to repopulate the new world. These traditions are too widespread and too similar in character to be mere coincidence. They definitely must represent semi-legendary recollections and reflections of some terrible cataclysm that shook the earth in its early days to its very foundations.

And the significant thing is that the main physical feature of this cataclysm, according to all the traditions, was water! A great world-destroying deluge is particularly significant in light of the fact that the sedimentary rocks of the geologic column, which contain the fossil record, were obviously nearly all laid down originally as sediments under moving water. As noted above, most of these must indeed have been deposited under *catastrophic* conditions, under floodwaters, or under correspondingly disturbed conditions beneath the ocean.

The Biblical record of the Flood of Noah, of course, supplies the only truly accurate record of this great cataclysm. If it truly occurred as recorded (under perfect divine inspiration, it should be noted), then the Flood was an overwhelming aqueous catastrophe which completely changed the antediluvian world (including its geography, geologic structure, and its meteorologic and hydrologic processes) and destroyed all dry-land animals except those preserved in the Ark. The Apostle Peter went so far as to say concerning it that "the *cosmos* that then was, being *cataclysmed* with water, perished" (II Peter 3:6), and the Lord Jesus Himself confirmed that "the *cataclysm* came and destroyed them *all*" (Luke 17:27).

The tremendous masses of sediments which must have been eroded and redeposited, the vast hordes of plants and animals trapped and buried in the sediments, the volcanic and tectonic upheavals, the changed climate and glaciations resulting, and other clearly implied aspects of the great Deluge provide a perfect framework of interpretation for most of the sedimentary strata of the earth's crust.

The usual order of deposition of fossils (as noted before, there are many, many exceptions to this *usual* order) would be such that the simpler fossils would be deposited near the bottom, and the more complex fossils near the top of each local geologic column. The hydrodynamic sorting action of moving water is quite efficient, so that each stratum would tend to contain an assemblage of fossils of similar shapes and sizes. Simple organisms, dwelling at the lower elevations, would normally also be buried at the lower elevations. More complex animals, larger and more mobile, and dwelling at higher levels, would obviously tend to be buried, if caught by the sediments at all, only at higher elevations. Very few birds, higher mammals, and especially men, would be overtaken and buried, but would usually float on the surface until consumed by scavengers or simply decomposed.

All of these implications of diluvial catastrophism are borne out by the actual character of the sedimentary rocks and their contained fossils. Details may be difficult to decipher at particular locations, but this basic framework is an adequate interpretive tool, and the difficulties of detail are far less serious than those entailed in the evolutionary and uniformitarian framework.

The fossil record does not at all testify to a billion-year history of evolutionary progress on the earth. Rather, when rightly understood, it speaks of a great divine judgment, of the sovereign power of a righteously angry Creator. More than anything else, the fossil record confirms the reality of *death* and therefore of sin and divine retribution, calling men even today to repentance before they perish in the future cataclysm of fire (II Peter 3:9, 10).

Chapter Four

THE CASE FOR CREATION

In previous chapters we have stressed the scientific weaknesses and fallacies of the asserted case for evolution. In this chapter we shall see, not only that there is no real evidence for evolution, but also that the testimony of true science is unequivocally and positively in favor of special creation.

We have acknowledged that most *scientists* believe in evolution, but this is not at all the same as saying that *science* teaches evolution. Scientists are people, and this means that they are fallible, sinful, prejudiced, selfish, and proud — just like all other people! Science, on the other hand, means *knowledge* — not theories, opinions, beliefs, or philosophies, but actual, verified, factual, certain *knowledge* — the organized body of observed data and experimentally verified processes and their interrelationships.

It is true that most scientists reject Biblical Christianity — just as do most lawyers and most plumbers and most ditch-diggers. This is not because of their science but because of their fallen natures which, as in all men, resist the demands of the Word of God.

There exists a minority of scientists, just as in every other walk of life, who *do* believe in Biblical Christianity, and this in itself confirms the fact that nothing in science, as such, compels a man to believe in evolution and its philosophy. For example, the Creation Research Society, organized only in 1963, has a regular membership of approximately three hundred scientists, each committed to belief in special creation as opposed to evolution, and each believing in Jesus Christ as personal Lord and Saviour.

Included among these three hundred creationist scientists are specialists in every branch of science, including many biologists, as well as physicists, chemists, geologists, archaeologists, and others. These men are all convinced that the data of their own scientific specialties favor belief in creation rather than evolution. Undoubtedly the number of creationist scientists not in the Society is much larger than the number of actual members. Thus, although creationists definitely represent a minority viewpoint among scientists, it is a significant minority. It is certainly true to say, therefore, that all the actual scientific data in *any* field of science are fully consistent with Biblical creationism. One's choice between evolutionism and creationism, then, is not really a scientific decision at all but rather a spiritual and moral decision. It is *easier* to be an evolutionist in the modern intellectual world (and this is the main reason why so many people accept evolution), but neither Biblical nor scientific *truth* is ever really determined by popular approval.

The Nature of Scientific Law

Science, in the proper sense, is the study and elucidation of present natural processes. Thus, chemistry deals with chemical processes, biology with biological processes, geology with geological processes. A particular scientific discipline involves the observation and measurement of the data of concern to that field, including how these data affect each other in the various processes through which they interact.

The essence of the "scientific method" is *experimental reproducibility*. That is, an experiment or measurement involving a particular process, if repeated later under the same conditions, will yield the same results. Thus, nature is basically predictable and therefore describable, provided one knows and can control all the different factors involved in the experiment.

It seems reasonable to assume that such processes have acted in the past, and will continue to act in the future, in much the same way they do now. However, it is also clear that we do not *know* that this is so. The assumption of uniformity, if it is a truly valid and universal principle, would obviously preclude the possibility of either a beginning or an end to the world and its processes. Basically, this leads to the so-called "steady-state" theory of the universe.

One may place his faith in such assumptions if he prefers to do so. However, it should be clear that these assumptions necessarily are outside the domain of true science. Science, as such, can deal only with present processes and not with the processes of the prehistoric past or the unknown future. The unlimited extrapolation of these processes of the present, on the basis of uniformitarianism, is not a bit more scientific or reasonable than the assumption of special creation in the past and a climactic termination in the future. Either approach is a matter of faith, not science.

However, the scientific study of present processes can certainly give an insight into which type of faith is more reasonable. And we shall see that science, in its true sense, clearly indicates special creation as the most probable explanation for things as they are.

Energy and Entropy

All real processes in the world — whether these processes are physical, biological, geological, or otherwise —
have certain features in common. They all involve phenomena occurring in space and time, and the phenomena
all involve the interplay of two profoundly important
entities known as energy and entropy.

Energy is a concept which is used to measure the
capacity of the phenomenon to accomplish "work." There
are many different kinds of energy, such as electrical
energy, light energy, sound energy, heat energy, and so
on. Even matter itself is basically one form of energy.
Thus everything in the real world is one form of energy
or another, and all processes in the world — that is, everything that "happens" — basically consist simply of transformations of energy from one kind into another.

The concept of entropy is used to measure the lack
of availability of the energy in a system. If the energy is
available and can be converted into useful work, the
entropy is low; if it is not available, the entropy is high.
Putting it in a different though equivalent way, entropy
is a measure of the state of disorder of a system. A
system which is highly organized and arranged, intricate
and complex, has a low entropy; one which has its com-
ponent parts disorganized and scattered about in a random fashion is one of high entropy. A brick building has
a low entropy; the same bricks scattered on the ground
after the building is wrecked have a high entropy.

Now all real processes in the world (and this includes
everything that happens) involve the interplay of energy
and entropy. Energy includes all phenomena, even matter itself, while entropy describes the "state" of all things.

It is thus profoundly significant that the most basic

laws of science, the laws which provide the universal framework within which all processes must operate, are the two laws which are associated respectively with energy and entropy. These are the famous First and Second Laws of Thermodynamics. In fact, they are commonly called by scientists simply the First Law and the Second Law.

These laws are based upon more evidence and are more universally applicable than any other principles in science. They have been confirmed by countless thousands of experiments on systems ranging in size from the nuclear to the astronomic, and there is no known exception to either of them.

The First Law, also called the Law of Energy Conservation, states that in any closed system no energy is either created or destroyed, though it can and does go through various kinds of transformations. The Second Law states that in any real process, in a closed system, the entropy must increase.

Thus the First Law confirms that no creation of energy (and this includes everything) is now taking place in the world, nor is anything being annihilated. The Second Law says that everything is becoming more and more disorganized; that the available energy for maintaining the physical processes of the universe is decreasing. Everything tends to become simpler, more random, more disordered. Things are getting old and wearing out. The universe is running down.

The philosophy of evolution is clearly refuted by these two basic and fundamental scientific laws. Evolution teaches that all things have been developed from primordial beginnings by means of present processes and thus that "creation" is continuous and is still continuing; the First Law, on the other hand, says that nothing is now being created and that nothing has been created in the past as long as this law has been in effect in the universe.

Similarly, evolution teaches that there is a universal tendency for things to become better organized, more complex, more highly specialized and adapted. The Second Law, contrariwise, recognizes a universal tendency toward disintegration, randomness, uselessness, decay and death.

It should be very plain that evolution and the Two Laws squarely contradict each other. According to evolution, the present processes which science studies must basically be processes of *innovation* and *integration*. According to the Two Laws, these processes rather are basically processes of *conservation* and *disintegration*.

These two opposing tendencies can, of course, be harmonized locally and temporarily in a so-called "open system," as distinguished from the "closed system" which we visualize in stating the laws of thermodynamics. That is, an excess inflow of "ordering energy" into the system from outside may cause it temporarily to grow and become more highly organized. Thus a crystal may grow for a while, a child may grow into an adult, or men may build a structure. But each of these, and all other illustrations of apparent decrease in entropy, are only local and temporary. The crystal eventually disintegrates, the man finally dies and the structure sooner or later falls into decay. Any such integrative process (not to say a "creative" process) is basically unnatural and requires provision of some extraordinary and continuing supply of "negative entropy" for its maintenance.

The evolutionist commonly ignores this problem. When confronted with it, he will usually say that the mechanism of mutation and natural selection provides the means of overcoming the Second Law and assuring the ongoing of evolutionary development. On the broader scale, he will say that the whole earth is an open system and that the excess energy for maintaining evolution as a worldwide process comes from the sun.

But these are mere equivocations. Mutations are themselves a perfect example of the Second Law. Since they represent random changes in highly ordered systems, they almost inevitably result in a decrease of organization and therefore a decrease in viability of the creatures (or species) experiencing them. Supposedly beneficial mutations, with a higher degree of organization, are so rare as to be utterly meaningless, if indeed they exist at all.

On the broad scale, it is true that the energy from the sun serves to maintain the various biological and physical processes on the earth. But the method or process by which this energy is supposedly converted into an evolutionary development on a global scale is utterly mysterious. Furthermore, to say that the evolutionary process even involves the sun means essentially that it must also involve the solar system, and therefore the galaxy, and therefore the whole universe. Thus evolution is a universal Law of Nature! Witness the present plethora of speculation about the evolution of life on planets in other galaxies. One of the most commonly cited justifications for the billions of dollars being poured into the space program is that we might learn more about the evolution of the universe and life on other worlds. But evolution simply cannot be true on such a cosmic scale if the Second Law of Thermodynamics is true (and it is!). Each is exactly the converse of the other. One is a hypothetical universal law of growth and progress: the other is a demonstrated universal law of decay and death.

To summarize, science in the true sense can deal only

with present processes. All these present processes operate within the framework of just two basic laws of conservation and decay. Since, therefore, present processes are not creative and integrative, they can really tell us nothing whatever about how the world was "created and made."

The only reasonable deduction from these scientific laws is that the world, with all its processes and with all its components, was brought into existence at some time in the past by means of creative and ordering processes which no longer exist and are therefore no longer available for scientific study. The First Law tells us either that the world has always existed in its present form or else that it was specially created at some time in the past. The Second Law tells us that it cannot always have existed in its present form or else it would already have completely disintegrated and died. The universe must have had a beginning, therefore, and that beginning must have been by special creation!

The Time of Creation

Since all processes are basically decay processes, they all involve certain transformations which proceed at certain rates from one form into another. When the decay rate of the process is known, and its results are available for measurement, then in principle it at first seems possible to calculate how long the particular process has been in operation. This kind of approach has been used to calculate dates for various events in the supposed geologic history of the earth and even the age of the earth itself.

However, the validity of all such age-estimates is directly dependent upon the assumption of uniformity — that is, that no change has ever occurred in the decay rate and that none of the decay products were actually brought into the system by special creation or by influx from outside. The assumption of uniformity is not legitimate, since there are many physical variables which affect *every* natural process, and past changes in any of these would affect the rate. The Second Law says that every process is basically a decay process, but says nothing about the *rate* of decay. It is never possible to *know* that the rate has never changed, no matter what the process may be. In fact, it is all but certain that all such rates change frequently and significantly as local conditions change.

Furthermore, in the light of the inferred necessity for special creation to bring all processes and their components originally into existence, it is reasonable that equilibrium amounts of both parent and daughter components would have been included in the creative act to begin with. Thus, the entire world would have been brought into existence as a fully functioning integrated whole, right from the beginning. Every portion of it would necessarily have an "appearance of age" at the very moment of its creation. Whatever this "apparent age" might be (as calculated on the basis of the assumptions of uniform process rates and no special creation) it would obviously have no necessary relation to its true age.

If any proposed method of estimating geologic time is examined critically on these two questions, it will invariably be found that the uniformitarian assumption is not only unprovable but also unreasonable. For any such method to be valid, it must be known that: (1) the rate of the particular process has never varied from what it is now measured to be; and (2) none of the apparent "product" of the process was ever introduced into the system from outside the process. Since there is no such thing in nature as an absolutely constant and inviolable process rate, and since there is no such thing in nature as a perfectly "closed system," it is quite obvious that neither assumption can be truly valid.

As an example of how the first assumption leads to fallacious results, consider the radiocarbon method. Radiocarbon is formed in the upper atmosphere by the interaction of incoming cosmic radiation with atoms of nitrogen. This radioactive isotope of carbon (Carbon 14) is identical chemically with ordinary carbon (Carbon 12), and so enters into all the normal chemical reactions associated with carbon dioxide in the life cycles of plants and animals. For the world as a whole, there is assumed to be a certain equilibrium ratio of radiocarbon atoms to normal carbon atoms, since the former gradually decay radioactively to offset the new radiocarbon continually being formed.

In the normal life cycle of an organism, carbon is continually being taken in and given out and thus every organism presumably contains the equilibrium amount of radiocarbon and natural carbon in its system. When it dies, however, it, of course, ceases to take any additional radiocarbon into its system, and the radiocarbon already present gradually decays at a known rate into normal carbon. Thus, if the ratio of radiocarbon to natural carbon is measured at some time after death, it will be smaller than the equilibrium amount in living organisms, and the actual time elapsed since death can be calculated on the basis of the known decay rate. This technique has been widely used during the past two decades to date events of supposedly the past 50,000 years .

Several processes are involved in this method of dating and all are subject to significant variations in rate. For example, the origin of the radiocarbon to begin with depends on the influx of cosmic radiation in the upper atmosphere and the accessibility of nitrogen atoms with which to react. It thus assumes that conditions in the earth's atmosphere have always been the same as now. However, evidence has accumulated in recent years that the earth's magnetic field may have been radically different in the past, and this may very well have repelled or diverted much of the cosmic radiation. An even more important possibility is that there was much more water vapor and carbon dioxide in the atmosphere in the past than at present, and these substances would have filtered out most of the cosmic rays before they could have formed Carbon 14 atoms.

This all means, of course, that the ratio of radiocarbon to normal carbon in the past was probably much less than at present. The radioactivity of an organism would therefore disappear after death more quickly than under the present equilibrium. If its "apparent age" were calculated on the basis of present equilibrium conditions and decay rates, it would appear much older than it really is.

With the establishment of present conditions in the upper atmosphere (presumably after the great Flood), it would take many centuries, or even millennia, for the present carbon equilibrium to be established on a world-wide basis with the amount of radiocarbon being formed in balance with the amount being lost through radioactive decay. Thus the discrepancy between the "true age" and the "radiocarbon age" would increase the further back in time the organism lived and died.

As an example of how the second assumption (that is, that the process has always been a "closed system," with no stage in the process affected by external factors) leads to invalid results, consider the uranium-lead method. As the radiocarbon method has been the chief technique used for dating "recent" events in earth history, so the uranium method has been the chief method for dating "ancient" events, and even the age of the earth itself, which is now supposed to be about five billion years.

Uranium is known to decay through a long chain of intermediate daughter products to a final stable isotope of lead. Since the present decay rates are known and are believed to be rather constant, the amount of radiogenic lead found in association with uranium in a mineral provides a means of calculating the apparent age of the deposit in which it is located.

However the mineral is not very likely to have remained a truly closed system during all the supposed hundreds of millions of years since its emplacement. Some of the uranium may have been leached out or some of the radiogenic lead may have been assimilated from external sources — both being very real possibilities physically and chemically — and either would make the apparent age immensely greater than the true age.

As a matter of fact, it is quite reasonable to say that some — perhaps all — of the radiogenic lead was in the mineral right from the beginning. If one admits the necessity — or even the possibility — of real *creation,* then the creation of all substances in equilibrium in a fully-completed, functioning universe is completely plausible.

This possibility becomes even more compelling when one considers the problem of the origin of the uranium itself. Most naturalistic cosmogonies begin with simple elements such as hydrogen and helium and then try to postulate some way in which the heavier elements could have "evolved" from the simpler. This type of process basically goes against the second law of thermodynamics, of course, and so requires the presence of tremendous external energies to make it possible.

Various theories have been proposed for the origin of the elements, but none has gained general acceptance and there seem thus far to be insuperable difficulties with all of them. Probably there is no real answer to this question except special creation itself.

Be that as it may, whether this process of "nucleogenesis" involved purely natural processes of integration under the impulse of the tremendous energies in the interior of a stellar furnace of some kind, or supernatural processes of creation and organization carried out by God Himself, it is plausible that all the elements would have been built up successively from the simplest hydrogen atom to the final uranium atom (and possibly even to the short-lived trans-uranium elements). When this process terminated, therefore, there would have been presumably more or less a continuous series of all elements present in some sort of decreasing order of magnitude.

It seems not at all unlikely, therefore, that certain amounts of lead (in all its isotopes), as well as other elements in the present decay chain, could have been associated with the uranium from the very time of its formation. Especially is this true if we recognize the necessity of a real creation of the elements in the beginning, — a necessity clearly invoked by the two laws of thermodynamics. The "apparent age" of a uranium-lead mineral, therefore, if we neglect this implied necessity of the creation of radiogenic lead as well as the uranium and all its intermediate products, must be immensely greater than its "true age."

Similar fallacies are implicit in all other commonly used methods of estimating geologic time. All methods ignore the probability of a real creation of some part of the components of the process as well as the possibility of subsequent change in the factors affecting the process rates.

Thus, the various geologic "ages" that are published from time to time are completely unreliable. They are based on the assumptions of uniformity and evolution and, since these assumptions are invalid, the age-estimates (except perhaps for those within the past few thousand years) are likewise invalid. It may be possible to derive some kind of relation eventually between the "apparent age" and the "true age," but, if this is possible at all, it must ultimately be based on divine revelation as to the "true age."

In the last analysis, we must finally conclude that if we are to know *anything* about creation — its date, processes, order, duration, or anything else — the Creator must tell us! Science cannot tell us, since science can deal only with present processes, and present processes are not creative processes. But this very fact, as we have seen, strongly argues for the fact of Creation sometime in the past.

If we expect to learn anything more than this about the Creation, then God alone can tell us. And He has told us! In the Bible, which is the Word of God, He has told us everything we *need* to know about the Creation and earth's primeval history. This is the record we shall consider in the final chapter.

Chapter Five

EVOLUTION AND THE BIBLE

The final and conclusive evidence against evolution is the fact that the Bible denies it. The Bible is the Word of God, absolutely inerrant and verbally inspired. The fact that some men do not believe this is no argument against it. The evidence supporting its claims, both internally and externally, is literally overwhelming to anyone who is willing, carefully and seriously, to consider it. This is not the place to discuss these evidences, and we are here simply assuming that the Bible is truly God's Word and that it is therefore completely true and authoritative, no matter what the subject may be with which it deals. And the Bible does, quite plainly and emphatically, reject the evolutionary explanation of origins.

As we have noted in the previous chapter, divine revelation is necessary if we are really to *know* anything about origins. The Bible gives us the revelation we need, and it will be found that all the known facts of science or history can be very satisfactorily understood within this Biblical framework.

Furthermore, let it be emphasized that the Biblical record of origins was written to be understood and therefore is to be taken literally rather than mystically or parabolically. There is no need for some special "key" of interpretation to be supplied by modern evolutionists (or, for that matter, by ancient evolutionists). The Biblical record of special creation of all things by an omnipotent personal God is unique among ancient cosmogonies. All other religions and philosophies of antiquity presupposed the eternality of matter and an essentially evolutionary development of the primeval chaos into the present cosmos. It would thus have been much easier for the early Israelites to comprehend an evolutionary cosmogony than the concept of special creation *ex nihilo*; and therefore Genesis 1 was written in plain, emphatic terminology, that they might clearly understand that the eternal God had called the entire physical universe into existence simply by His own Word, and had then "made" or organized it into its present form in six days.

Integrity of the Record

The first chapter of Genesis (including the first three verses of Genesis 2) clearly professes to be the revelation that God has given man concerning the origin of all things. It opens with the incomparable statement: "In the beginning God created the heavens and the earth."

Then, after outlining the creation and development of all the inorganic and organic components of the physical universe, including man himself, the account concludes with the summary in Genesis 2:1-3: "Thus the heavens and the earth were finished, and all the host of them. And on the seventh day God ended his work which he had made; and he rested on the seventh day from all his work which he had made. And God blessed the seventh day, and sanctified it: because that in it he had rested from all his work which God created and made."

Many people have tried to explain away the record of this chapter by calling it an allegory, or hymn, or myth. But this is impossible without simultaneously undermining the integrity of all the rest of the Bible. This first chapter of Genesis fits perfectly into the historical record of the rest of the book of Genesis, which in turn is foundational to the entire Bible.

The second, third, and fourth chapters amplify the outline in Chapter One, especially as it relates to man, and then describe the developments immediately following the Creation. The rest of Genesis describes in chronological form the events of early history down to the establishment of the nation of Israel and its exile in Egypt. The rest of the Bible, especially the New Testament frequently quotes from, and alludes to, the book of Genesis, including its earliest chapters. If the early chapters of Genesis are not historical and correct, there is no escaping the conclusion that Paul and Peter and the other writers of the New Testament, were guilty of either ignorance or misrepresentation when they cited these events as true and as, in fact, foundational in the entire plan of salvation.

Especially significant is the fact that the Lord Jesus Christ Himself frequently quoted from Genesis. In one instance He used a quotation from both Genesis 1 and Genesis 2 (Matthew 19:4-6), thus stamping these chapters as both historically accurate and divinely inspired.

Thus, one cannot legitimately question the historicity of the creation record without questioning the judgment or veracity of the Apostles and of Christ Himself. And this, of course, is an option which is not open to any consistent Christian.

The Nature of Creation

Granted, then, that the creation account is to be accepted as historically accurate and as divinely inspired, the problem then remains to determine what it actually says concerning creation.

Probably the most important aspects of creation as revealed are that it was *perfect* and that it was *complete*. Six times (Gen. 1:4, 10, 12, 18, 21, 25) God evaluated His handiwork as "good." Finally, after everything was finished, we read: "God saw everything that he had made, and, behold, it was very good" (Gen. 1:31).

This can only mean that, in the judgment of an omniscient and holy God, there was nothing in either the methods or results of His creation which involved disorder, struggle, predation, decay, or death. All things were in perfect harmony and order.

The fact of the *completedness* of creation is emphasized again and again in Genesis 2:1-3, as well as in Exodus 20:11, Hebrews 4:3, 10, and other Scriptures. Thus, nothing is now being "created" or "made" (Gen. 2:3). The processes of nature by which God now *sustains* His creation are thus entirely different from those by which He first produced it. Present-day physical and biological processes, which are, of course, the only processes available for scientific measurement and study, therefore can tell us nothing whatever about the processes God used in creating and making all things. His "creative" acts consisted of calling the physical universe into existence (Gen. 1:1), of calling animal life into existence (Gen. 1:21), and of calling human life in His own image (Gen. 1:27) into existence. His "making" acts consisted of organizing and arranging the created materials into their final states of high order and perfection.

We have already seen that the two basic laws of science testify that nothing is *now* being "created" or "organized." The two laws of thermodynamics are statements of *conservation* and of *disintegration*. They thus add their testimony to that of the Bible to the effect that the creation and ordering of all things must have been accomplished by entirely different processes from those which now prevail in the world.

This fact is exactly in contradiction to the theory of evolution. Evolution contends that the present processes of nature can account for the development of all things in the universe from primordial beginnings to their present conditions. Thus "creation" in the evolutionary sense is still going on, and there is a universal tendency toward greater complexity and perfection.

Furthermore, evolution supposedly involves billions of years of struggle and death as the very agency of evolution, through "natural selection" and "survival of the fittest." Such a condition cannot be reconciled with the statement of God that all things were "very good" at the end of the creation period.

Thus the Biblical testimony of completeness and of perfection at the end of creation clearly refutes the evolutionary philosophy. Furthermore, the Biblical record of the fall of man and God's curse on the earth (Gen. 3:17-19) accounts not only for the existence of struggle and death in the present world, but also for the universal tendency toward decay as enunciated in the second law of thermodynamics.

Finally, and almost incidentally, the ten-times-repeated phrase "after its kind" in Genesis 1:11-25 emphasizes the fact that organic evolution was not utilized as a process of creation. Whatever biologic unit may have been signified by the "kind," it obviously specifies the outside limits of such biologic variation permitted by the complex genetic structures as originally created.

Evolution, to the contrary, maintains a continuity of all forms of life, so that all organisms basically are related by descent from a common ancestor. This concept is refuted not only by Genesis but also by the New Testament. The Apostle Paul clearly states (I Cor. 15:38, 39) that "all flesh is *not* the same flesh," and that God has given "to every seed its own body."

The Duration of Creation

Since the creation and ordering of all things could not have been accomplished by the processes of the present cosmos, it should be obvious that these processes can tell us nothing whatever about the creation. As already noted, if we want to know anything about creation — the duration, the processes, the order, or anything else, only God can tell us about them. Science cannot do it since science can deal only with present processes, and present processes are not creative processes.

And God has *told* us! He has said, as plainly as it could possibly be said, that He created and made all things in *six days!* The reason why He took six days instead of only the twinkling of an eye to do this was in order for His work-week of six days to serve as a pattern for man's work-week of six days. This is made perfectly clear in Genesis 2:1-3 and Exodus 20:9-11.

That these "days" are solar days is evident not only from the parallel of the divine and human work-weeks but also from the fact that the term normally means solar days unless the context clearly indicates a parabolic sense. The Hebrew for "day" (*yom*) may occasionally be used to mean an indefinite time, but it *never* means a definite circumscribed time period (such as bounded by "evening" and "morning," or as implied by the "first" day, "second" day, etc.) unless that time period be an *actual* day. Similarly, the Hebrew plural for "days" (*yamim*) is never used in Scripture for any time period except literal days. For these and numerous other reasons it is necessary to conclude that God's entire work of creating and making this physical universe and everything in it was accomplished in six solar days. As if to settle beforehand the questions that might later be raised, God in fact actually defined the word "day" the very first time it was used (Gen. 1:5) where it is said that "God called the light Day, . . . and the evening and the morning were the first day."

The record does not tell us what the source of light may have been for the first three days. The fact of the earth's axial rotation is implied, however, by the successive periods of light and darkness, and by the statement that each "day," or "period of light," was terminated by an "evening" and a "morning." Whatever this initial light-source may have been, on the fourth day the light was concentrated, as it were, in two great "light-bearers," one to rule the "day" and one to rule the night. It is plain throughout the entire record of creation that the term "day " is continuously employed to mean the period of light in the diurnal rotation of the earth on its axis. Such a meaning as "age" or "geologic period" is utterly alien to the context.

Serious theological difficulties are also inherent in the so-called "day-age" theory. Most serious is the fact that identification of the geological ages with the days of creation necessarily requires that disorder, decay, suffering and death must have existed in the world long before Adam's sin and God's Curse on the earth. This, in effect, makes God the author of confusion and calls evil "good," and is, of course, explicitly contradicted by Scripture (Gen. 1:31; 3:17; Rom. 5:12; 8:20-22; I Cor. 15:21).

This same difficulty exists with the so-called "gap theory," which would place the five-billion-year history of the geological ages (with all their evidences of struggle and suffering and death, and with the evolutionary progress supposedly resulting from these processes) in an imagined interval between the first two verses of Genesis. On the basis of the standard system of geological ages, man himself appears in the last one or two million years of the record, so that the gap theory entails the very serious theological problem of "pre-Adamite" men, with numerous appearances of culture and even religion, but evidently with no knowledge of the gospel or of salvation. The Bible, of course, not only is completely silent with respect to any such pre-Adamite men, but explicitly emphasizes that Adam was the *first* man (I Cor. 15:45).

Thus, no compromise with the geological ages and the fossil record which provides the basis for their very identification, is Scripturally feasible. The fossils must have been buried *after* (not *before* or *during*) the six days of creation.

The objection, of course, has been raised that the universe looks as though it must have taken far longer than six days to produce. It should be remembered, however, that this appearance of great age is based on the assumption that the world must have been brought into its present form by present processes. And this assumption is refuted both by Scripture and the two laws of thermodynamics.

Since creation actually was accomplished by processes entirely different from those now existing, it is clear that the "apparent age" of the world has no necessary correlation with its "true age." Real creation obviously requires creation with an "appearance of age." Thus, Adam was made as a full-grown man, the newly formed trees had fruit on them, the light from the stars could be seen on earth at the moment of their creation, and so on. If anything is ever truly *created,* it necessarily must look initially as though it had a prior existence, and therefore it has an appearance of some "age," if that "age" is conceived in terms of present processes.

The Date of Creation

The date of creation is not necessarily the traditional Ussher date of 4004 B.C., of course. Nevertheless, it should be recognized that the general method of Ussher — that of relying on the Biblical data alone — is the only proper approach to determining the date of creation. The genealogies in Genesis 5 and 11 provide the most strategic data in this connection. If these are taken at face value, they indicate that Ussher must have been correct at least in order of magnitude.

It is true that different ancient versions have somewhat different numbers in the genealogical lists. It is also true that the chronology of the historical period, to which these genealogies are tied at the beginning of Israel's history, is far from settled as to exact dates and durations.

It may even be true that there are gaps in one or both of the genealogical lists in Genesis 5 and 11. That is, it is conceivable that the lists represent only the more prominent names in the ancestry of Abraham rather than the full lineage. If such gaps exist, however, they must be of relatively small magnitude; otherwise the lists become pointless and might as well have been omitted altogether.

Because of the above reasons, the exact date of creation cannot be determined with any confidence. On the other hand, even after allowing as much time as reasonably warranted for all these uncertainties, it still remains true that the Biblical record indicates creation to have taken place only a few thousands of years ago. The possible range of uncertainty may be to about 15,000 years ago, with a more likely upper limit of not more than 10,000 years ago. In fact, there is nothing really impossible or unreasonable about the traditional date of 4004 B.C.

The Biblical Framework of Earth History

It may help in summarizing our consideration of the evolution question to outline the major events of earth history as revealed in Scripture. It will be found, if enough serious study is devoted to it, that all legitimate data of true science and history can be understood within this framework. It is not at all necessary to postulate a great age for the universe and an evolutionary development of all things to their present state as is required by the evolution concept. The Biblical framework is as follows:

(1) A Six-Day Period of Special Creation

During these six days, all things were created and made. God was employing creative and integrative processes during this period in contrast to the conservative and disintegrative processes which prevail in the present order. At the end of this period, God's universe was both *complete* and *perfect,* with all its components functioning together in maximum order and harmony, and thus necessarily having a large "apparent age" in relation to present processes.

(2) The Fall and Curse

As a result of the introduction of spiritual disorder into the universe — first by Satan in heaven and then by man on earth — God pronounced His curse on man's dominion, introducing a universal principle of increasing physical disorder, decay, and death into the world. (Note Gen. 3:17-19; Rom. 5:12; 8:20-22; I Cor. 15:21, 22). This principle, superimposed on the basic principle of conservation by which all things are upheld and sustained by God (Col. 1:17; Heb. 1:3; II Peter 3:5, 7) is unnatural and will be removed from the cosmos when Christ returns (II Peter 3:13; Rev. 21:4; 22:3; Rom. 8:21).

Thus, the end of the Creation period marked the beginning of the application of the universal conservation principle to the earth's processes, and the curse marked the introduction of the universal tendency toward disorder in these processes. These principles are now formalized scientifically as the first and the second laws of thermodynamics and provide the framework within which all processes must function.

(3) *The Universal Deluge*

The form of the earth's surface and atmosphere, and the rates of action of most or all of the earth's processes, were drastically changed during the year of the great Flood of Noah. As the Apostle Peter says, "The world (Greek, *kosmos*) that then was, being overflowed (Greek, *katakluzo*) with water, perished" (II Peter 3:6).

Although the two basic Laws were, of course, not modified during this period, the *rates* of decay of many of the various processes in nature were caused to accelerate for a time. Because of the wholly universal and abnormal wickedness of men in those days, the tendency toward decay and death was abnormally increased, and the whole world of air-breathing creatures perished! Great volumes of sediments were eroded, transported and deposited, and vast hordes of animals and men were destroyed, with many undoubtedly being trapped and buried in the sediments. The earth's geography, geology, and meteorology were found to be profoundly changed when the human and animal occupants of Noah's Ark emerged from their shelter after the Flood.

Within the framework of these three great events of history — Creation, the Fall, and the Flood — can be explained all the data of true science and history. All the various evidences for evolution, as discussed in previous chapters, can be much better understood in terms of creationism and catastrophism.

There is thus neither need nor justification for the modern Christian to feel pressured into compromise with the prevalent evolutionary philosophy of these days with all of its attendant ills and evil influences. For he knows Christ, "in whom are hid all the treasures of wisdom and knowledge" (Col. 2:3); and He it is who is both Creator and Redeemer of the world.

Spiritual and Personal Implications of Evolution

If evolution were merely a biological theory, we would not need to be overly concerned about it. However, it is really a powerful religious faith and thus necessarily assumes great importance to the Bible-believing Christian, whose faith it seriously challenges.

Evolution is fundamentally a cosmogony without God, that philosophy which enables man to explain the origin and meaning of all things without a divine Creator and Sovereign of the universe. It postulates a universal naturalistic principle of development, of increase in organization and complexity, of progress from primeval chaos to ultimate perfection. Through the evolutionary perspective, man views himself as the highest attainment of the cosmic process. He has not only managed to decipher the meaning of the historical record of evolutionary progress, but now believes himself able even to plan and control future evolution.

On the personal level, a man committed to an evolutionary faith will thus, if he is consistent, either become a disciple of social changes calculated to advance the social order or else immerse himself in selfish pursuits of his own, sensing his personal futility as an individual in the cosmic process.

Biblical Christianity, on the other hand, gives dignity and purpose to life. When a person, in faith, recognizes God as Creator, he then knows also that there is meaning in his own personal existence. Though he knows there is something missing in the relationship he now has to his Creator, he nevertheless knows that somehow God must have had reason for causing him to be.

Having come thus far, he should now see that such a God would reveal Himself to those of His creatures truly desiring to know Him and to find His purpose for their own lives. And he will then find in the Bible that very revelation he seeks.

The Bible says nothing of an age-long struggle upward from chaos. Rather, it tells of an originally perfect Creation of a perfectly-ordered cosmos, marred later by sin and God's curse on man and his dominion. It explains the unsatisfactory nature of his relationship with God to be the result of his own sinful nature, as well as his consequent sinful thoughts and deeds. But it also tells of God's love for him and His desire to reconcile him to Himself. It tells how God, in the person of His Son, bore the penalty of his sins, suffering and dying on a cross, in order to redeem and save men who deserved to die but whom He loved and desired to save.

The theory of evolution is, if rightly understood, nothing but "bad news," a delusion of Satan, offering an illusory Utopia for the race in some long-distant age but only meaningless existence and imminent death for the individual in the present. But the message of the Bible is "good news," the *gospel* of Jesus Christ, offering forgiveness and eternal life, as well as meaning and purpose for the present life, to every person who responds in faith to Him as Creator and Saviour and Lord.

Suggestions for Further Reading

To make for easier reading, no documentation has been included in the text of this book. On the other hand, critical readers may understandably hesitate to accept the full position advocated without such documentation. Accordingly, reference is made here to a number of other books, which are developed from essentially the same viewpoint, in which this has been provided. Only books are listed which are still in print.

I. *Books by the Same Author.*
Each of these may be obtained from the Presbyterian and Reformed Publishing Co., P.O. Box 185, Nutley, New Jersey 07110 and/or Baker Book House, 1019 Wealthy St., S.E., Grand Rapids, Michigan 49506.

> *The Genesis Flood.* (With John C. Whitcomb, Jr.), 1961 (Tenth Printing, 1967), 518 pp. $6.95.
>
> > The Biblical exposition of the Flood and its universality, together with an analysis of its geological and other scientific implications; refutation of the supposed paleontological evidences for evolution, with a critique of methods of geologic dating and related problems; a defense of Biblical creationism and catastrophism and refutation of evolutionary uniformitarianism.
>
> *The Twilight of Evolution.* 1963 (Seventh Printing, 1967). 103 pp. Cloth Edition $2.95. Paperback Edition $1.50.
>
> > A brief study of the evolutionary philosophy and its implications in every area of modern life, demonstrating that evolution is actually impossible scientifically and that special creation provides the only

69

realistic explanation of the physical data; the theological implications of evolution and its ultimate demise.

Studies in the Bible and Science. 1966 (Second Printing 1967) 186 pp. Cloth Edition $3.50. Paperback Edition $1.95.

Biblical and scientific studies of a variety of topics and issues in the general field of Christian evidences and Biblical creationism.

II. *Books by Other Authors.*

Clark, Harold W., *Fossils, Flood and Fire,* (Escondido, Calif., Outdoor Pictures, 1968).

A detailed study of the geologic effects of the flood and their relation to present geologic formations.

Clark, Robert T. and Bales, James D., *Why Scientists Accept Evolution* (Grand Rapids, Baker Book House, 1966), 113 pp.

A demonstration that factors other than scientific reasons have invariably influenced even the originators and leaders of evolutionary thought to become evolutionists.

Cook, Melvin A., *Prehistory and Earth Models* (London, Max Parrish Co., 1966), 353 pp.

Detailed critique of radioactivity and other methods of geochronometry, written by a Yale Ph.D. physical chemist with extensive experience in explosives and geophysics; scientific evidence of the earth's young age.

Cousins, Frank W., *Fossil Man* (Hants, England, Evolution Protest Movement, 1966), 106 pp.

A thorough discussion of all the important fossil

discoveries of supposed significance in theories of human evolution, with a demonstration of their fallacies; evidence that true man antedates supposedly more primitive types of "proto-men."

Custance, Arthur C., *Doorway Papers* (Published by author, Box 1283, Sta. B., Ottawa, Canada).

A series of about 35 fascinating, often provocative, booklets by a Christian anthropologist and linguist, supporting creationism in different fields.

DeWit, J. J. Duyvene, *A New Critique of the Transformist Principle in Evolutionary Biology* (Kampen, Netherlands, J. H. Kok, N. V., 1964), 62 pp.

A philosophical and biological criticism of evolution, by the recently deceased Head of the Zoology Department in the University of Orange Free State.

Kerkut, G. A., *Implications of Evolution* (New York, Pergamon Press, 1960), 174 pp.

A detailed analysis and criticism of all the supposed scientific evidences of evolution, written by one who is himself a prominent evolutionist.

Klotz, John W., *Genes, Genesis and Evolution* (St. Louis, Concordia Publishing House, 1955), 575 pp.

A thorough study of the biological and genetic evidences for and against the theory of evolution, showing the greater reasonableness of creationism, written by a Ph.D. biologist.

Lammerts, Walter E. (Editor), *Quarterly Journal of the Creation Research Society* (Ann Arbor, Michigan).

A periodical devoted to scientific articles supporting Biblical creationism and catastrophism.

Marsh, Frank L., *Life, Man and Time* (Escondido, Calif., Outdoor Pictures, Rev. Ed., 1967), 238 pp.

A convincing refutation of evolution and discussion of the true history of the earth by the Professor of Biology in Andrews University.

Shute, Evan, *Flaws in the Theory of Evolution* (Nutley, N. J., Craig Press, 1966), 286 pp.

A noted Canadian surgeon provides detailed refutations of the so-called evidences for evolution as well as many striking indications of creative design in nature.

Tilney, A. G. (Editor), *The Case against Evolution* (Hants, England, Evolution Protest Movement, 1964).

A compendium of about 100 papers by various authors, many of them eminent British scientists, refuting evolutionism.

Whitcomb, John C., Jr., *The Origin of the Solar System,* (Nutley, N. J., Presbyterian and Reformed Publ. Co., 1964), 34 pp.

A demonstration that no theory except special creation can account for the origin of the solar system, together with a refutation of the so-called "two-revelations" theory.

Young, Edward J., *Studies in Genesis One* (Philadelphia, Presbyterian and Reformed Publishing Co., 1964), 105 pp.

A detailed exegesis of the first chapter of Genesis, by one of the nation's foremost Hebrew scholars, showing that it must be understood historically and chronologically, not symbolically or allegorically.

Zimmerman, Paul A. (Editor), *Darwin, Evolution and Creation* (St. Louis, Concordia Publishing House, 231 pp.), 1959.

Studies on the influence and the scientific fallacies of Darwinism, by four Lutheran scholars.